WORLD WAR II

WORLD WAR II IN THE PACIFIC

BY ANGELA LIM

CONTENT CONSULTANT
Annika A. Culver, Ph.D.
Professor of East Asian History, Florida State University
Scholar, US-Japan Network for the Future

Cover image: In 1943, US aircraft returned to attack Japanese forces at Wake Island two years after the Battle of Wake Island.

Core Library

An Imprint of Abdo Publishing
abdobooks.com

abdobooks.com

Published by Abdo Publishing, a division of ABDO, PO Box 398166, Minneapolis, Minnesota 55439.

Printed in the United States of America, North Mankato, Minnesota.
052024
092024

THIS BOOK CONTAINS RECYCLED MATERIALS

Cover Photo: AP Images
Interior Photos: Niday Picture Library/Alamy, 4–5; Keystone/Hulton Archive/Getty Images, 7, 43; Bettmann/Getty Images, 9, 34–35, 36; Scherl/Sueddeutsche Zeitung Photo/Alamy, 12–13; PhotoQuest/Archive Photos/ Getty Images, 16–17; Underwood Archives/Archive Photos/Getty Images, 19; Hulton Archive/Archive Photos/Getty Images, 24–25; Joe Rosenthal/Photo 12/Universal Images Group/Getty Images, 27, 45; Corbis Historical/Getty Images, 29; Red Line Editorial, 31, 39

Editor: Marley Richmond
Series Designer: Ryan Gale

Library of Congress Control Number: 2023949025

Publisher's Cataloging-in-Publication Data

Names: Lim, Angela, author.
Title: World war II in the Pacific / by Angela Lim
Description: Minneapolis, Minnesota: Abdo Publishing, 2025 | Series: World war II | Includes online resources and index.
Identifiers: ISBN 9781098293697 (lib. bdg.) | ISBN 9798384912965 (ebook)
Subjects: LCSH: World War, 1939-1945--Juvenile literature. | Pacific Area--Juvenile literature. | World War, 1939-1945--Naval operations--Juvenile literature. | Military campaigns--Juvenile literature. | Politics and government--Juvenile literature.
Classification: DDC 940.53--dc23

CONTENTS

CHAPTER ONE

ATTACK ON PEARL HARBOR

Although it was early in the morning of December 7, 1941, the US naval base at Pearl Harbor on the Hawaiian island of Oahu was already bustling with activity. The United States was not yet involved in World War II (1939–1945). But fighting raged in Europe. Meanwhile, the Empire of Japan was active in the Pacific. The empire's Marines and Imperial Japanese Navy (IJN) were fighting to gain more territory. This concerned US military officials. Many feared that US involvement in the war was on the horizon.

Before it was attacked, the US naval base at Pearl Harbor housed many fuel tanks, submarines, and battleships.

December 7 began like any other day. Around the base, people crewed battleships. Other military members performed inspections and maintenance on these ships. The fleet docked at Pearl Harbor included nearly 100 vessels.

Radar operators kept watch on their equipment. A soldier got a ping on his system at 7:02 a.m. Aircraft were seen approaching Pearl Harbor. But the base was expecting US planes to arrive on the island later that day. Activities continued as usual.

Soon it became clear that something was horribly wrong. Hundreds of Japanese planes streaked through the sky and began dropping bombs on the base. For people at Pearl Harbor, the attack was a complete surprise. Military personnel scrambled toward their battle stations. But it was too late to fend off the attack.

For more than two hours, bombs rained down on the base. A huge torpedo struck the warship USS *Arizona*, causing it to explode. As ships sank, oil spilled into the ocean and caught on fire.

The USS *Shaw* was one of the destroyers hit by Japanese bombs during the attack on Pearl Harbor.

Around 10:00 a.m., Japanese pilots began to retreat. The attack killed more than 2,400 Americans. It was a huge success for Japan. Japanese military officials were planning to invade new territories in the Pacific. They didn't want the United States to interfere, so they attacked a US base first. While the United States' attention was focused on Pearl Harbor, Japanese forces advanced to their other targets.

PERSPECTIVES

THE ROLE OF OIL

US-Japan relations had been worsening long before the attack on Pearl Harbor. Japan had invaded and taken over European nations' colonies in the Pacific. Concerned with the growth of Japanese power, the United States placed an embargo on the empire. The United States would no longer trade oil with Japan. Japan is an island nation. It relies on trade for many important resources. As a result of the embargo, Japan lost access to 94 percent of its oil resources. Many historians believe this was a major reason for the Pearl Harbor attack. Japan would need to capture oil-rich areas. But first it would need to distract or disable the US military so the United States could not retaliate.

ENTERING THE WAR

The attack on Pearl Harbor shocked the United States from its neutral position in World War II. Just one day after the attack, Congress declared war on Japan. The United States officially entered World War II on December 8, 1941. It would be nearly four bloody years before the war in the Pacific came to an end.

World War II was divided into two fronts. Battles in the

US president Franklin D. Roosevelt signed the United States' declaration of war against Japan the day after Pearl Harbor was attacked.

European theater had begun in 1939. The battles against Japan made up the Pacific theater. Japan, Germany, and Italy were allies in World War II. They were the major countries of the Axis powers. The United States also declared war on Germany on December 11, 1941. Soon after, US troops were sent to Europe to fight in the European theater of the war. The United

INCARCERATION CAMPS

Negative opinions toward people of Japanese descent increased in the United States after the attack on Pearl Harbor. Some Americans began questioning whether Japanese Americans were loyal to the United States. On February 19, 1942, President Franklin D. Roosevelt signed an executive order that allowed the US military to relocate Japanese Americans from their homes. More than 100,000 Japanese Americans were forced to live in incarceration camps, which were sometimes called internment camps. These camps were meant to prevent Japanese Americans from passing information to Japan. Many sites had poor living conditions with cramped rooms and no running water.

States had joined the United Kingdom and the Soviet Union as a powerful member of the Allied powers.

The Japanese military's resolve tested the US military. Warfare evolved as aircraft carriers became crucial to victory. These large ships carry planes that can take off and land on their decks. Other advances in technology and science gave the United States the edge against a tough opponent that would not surrender easily.

STRAIGHT TO THE SOURCE

On December 8, 1941, President Franklin D. Roosevelt gave a speech before Congress, describing the attack on Pearl Harbor. He said:

> *Yesterday, December 7, 1941—a date which will live in infamy—the United States of America was suddenly and deliberately attacked by naval and air forces of the Empire of Japan. . . . I assert that we will not only defend ourselves to the uttermost but will make it very certain that this form of treachery shall never again endanger us.*

Source: "Speech by Franklin D. Roosevelt, New York (Transcript), 1941." *Library of Congress*, n.d., loc.gov. Accessed 4 Aug. 2023.

CONSIDER YOUR AUDIENCE

Adapt this passage for a different audience, such as your principal or friends. Write a speech conveying this same information for the new audience. How does your post differ from the original text and why?

CHAPTER TWO

EARLY JAPANESE VICTORIES

The Empire of Japan's military power had begun increasing in the late 1800s, long before World War II. The country became an empire after successes in wars, including World War I (1914–1918). With these victories, Japan gained territory in East Asia and the Pacific. The Japanese government believed it had the power to replace the United States as the major force in this area. The attack on Pearl Harbor was the empire's first direct challenge to the US military.

Japanese soldiers marched in a parade, holding the Rising Sun Flag. This flag was used by the Empire of Japan.

PERSPECTIVES

SURPRISE ATTACK

The Pearl Harbor attack was led by Japanese admiral Yamamoto Isoroku. Yamamoto did not think Japan could gain territories in the Pacific unless the potential for US involvement was eliminated. Yamamoto also did not think Japan could beat the United States in a long war. Therefore, he thought a surprise attack would force a quick surrender.

BATTLE OF WAKE ISLAND

The attack on Pearl Harbor prevented the US Navy from responding immediately to further Japanese advances. Only hours after the Pearl Harbor attack, Japan's military invaded Hong Kong and the Philippines. The IJN also immediately turned its attention to the US Marine Corps base at Wake Island, a US territory in the Pacific. Japanese pilots bombed the base for about two weeks. The attack destroyed US planes and ships.

Additionally, on December 11, 1941, a large fleet of Japanese naval ships approached Wake Island. Japan planned to overrun the island. The US Marine Corps was greatly outnumbered. Japanese forces expected a quick victory.

But the US marines were tough. They used coastal-defense guns to sink two Japanese destroyers. Several other Japanese ships were struck too. The IJN was forced to retreat and return later with more ships.

The Battle of Wake Island eventually ended with a Japanese victory on December 23. But it was not an easy success. The battle showed the strength and strategy of the US military. The marines' ability to temporarily hold off the Japanese strengthened Americans' spirits. The fighting at Wake Island proved that the United States would not give up easily.

DOUGLAS MACARTHUR

General Douglas MacArthur was a US Army commander. After the attack on Pearl Harbor, MacArthur led a group of US and Filipino soldiers against Japanese forces in the Philippines. The Japanese military forced MacArthur's troops to retreat, and US forces surrendered in April 1942. But MacArthur's bravery in the Philippines won him the Medal of Honor in 1942.

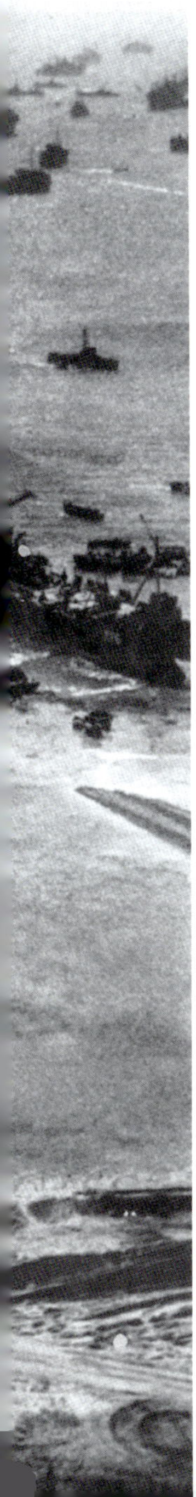

CHAPTER THREE

TURNING TIDES

With the element of surprise, the Empire of Japan secured victories at Pearl Harbor and Wake Island. Fighting continued in 1942 as the Japanese and US militaries clashed in the Pacific. The battles were not easy victories for either side. Thousands of American and Japanese soldiers lost their lives. The war tested the firepower and strategies of both nations.

During World War II, the US Navy's fleet grew from about 700 ships to more than 6,000.

THE BATTLE OF THE CORAL SEA

On May 4, 1942, a fleet of Japanese ships steered toward Port Moresby, the capital of Papua New Guinea. The port and its airfields were located along the Coral Sea, which is near Australia. The Japanese military wanted to capture Port Moresby from Australia, which was an ally of the United States. Then Japan could use the location as an air base. Japanese military officials could send their own planes from the base to invade Australia. The planes could also be used to defend Japanese territories in the Pacific.

Unlike earlier battles in the Pacific, the United States was prepared for the Battle of the Coral Sea. The US military had learned about Japanese plans for the attack. Two US aircraft carriers, the USS *Lexington* and the USS *Yorktown*, were stationed near the port. US pilots planned to fly aircraft from these ships as the Japanese advanced.

Japanese planes destroyed the USS *Lexington*. They also damaged the USS *Yorktown*, forcing the

The USS *Lexington* was hit by Japanese bombs during the Battle of the Coral Sea. Sailors and marines climbed down ropes over the side of the aircraft carrier to escape the sinking ship.

carrier to retreat to Pearl Harbor. Meanwhile, US planes sank a small Japanese aircraft carrier and inflicted heavy damage on a larger carrier called the *Shokaku*. Japanese rear admiral Takagi Takeo ordered his troops to retreat on May 8 because of those damages.

The Battle of the Coral Sea was the first time that the US military prevented the further advance of the Japanese. It stopped the Japanese from taking over Port Moresby and gaining a foothold near Australia. Furthermore, the damages to Japanese aircraft carriers gave an edge to the US Navy in other major battles in the Pacific. Although both sides of the battle suffered losses, the US military was better prepared than Japan for the battles to come.

THE BATTLE OF MIDWAY

The Midway Islands are a group of small islands about 1,300 miles (2,100 km) northwest of Honolulu, Hawaii. They were a US territory. The United States had maintained an air base and submarine base at Midway since 1941. Japan wanted to gain control of the Midway Islands because of their proximity to Pearl Harbor. A failure to defeat Japan at Midway would likely force the United States to surrender.

During World War II, military officials communicated over radio to coordinate attacks and strategize. However, their messages could be intercepted by the opposing side. To prevent information from falling into enemy hands, militaries used coded messages. If opponents intercepted a message, they would not be able to understand its contents. Japan and the United States both used codes during World War II.

US code breakers cracked the Japanese code. They learned that the IJN was planning to attack Midway. US admiral Chester Nimitz prepared to defend the islands. He stationed a fleet of ships 350 miles (560 km) northeast of Midway. The fleet included the freshly repaired USS *Yorktown*, two other aircraft

USS *YORKTOWN*

Japanese military officials believed that the USS *Yorktown* had been sunk in the Battle of the Coral Sea. Though heavily damaged, the aircraft carrier was able to return to Pearl Harbor for repairs. Initial assessments showed that it would take about three months for the repairs to be completed. But Admiral Nimitz commanded the crew to have the aircraft carrier repaired in three days. The maintenance crew succeeded, and the USS *Yorktown* set sail for Midway just three days later.

carriers, and several destroyers and cruisers. On June 3, 1942, US pilots took off from the aircraft carriers to collect information about Japanese positions. Japanese forces attacked one US aircraft.

Early the following morning, Japanese aircraft bombed Midway. The bombing severely damaged the base, but Yamamoto did not know that there were US ships nearby. When Japanese pilots turned around to refuel, Nimitz ordered his forces to attack. US pilots took off from aircraft carriers once again. They dropped bombs and torpedoes from their planes.

Because of the code breaking,

PERSPECTIVES

VICTORY AT MIDWAY

Many historians describe Midway as a turning point in World War II. While the battle showed the strength of US airpower, military officials involved in war strategy called the success a "victory of intelligence." Code breaking was a major reason for the victory. US military officials also carefully stationed the US fleet to launch an attack and located Japanese forces beforehand.

the US military was able to successfully defend Midway and make Japanese forces retreat on June 6. The Battle of Midway was a major US victory. It turned the tides of World War II in the Pacific. It stopped Japan's advance through the Pacific and put the empire on the defensive.

The victory at Midway marked a turning point for the United States. But World War II in the Pacific was far from over. The war continued for several years. Neither side showed signs of backing down.

FURTHER EVIDENCE

Chapter Three describes key aspects of the Battle of Midway. What is one of the main points of this chapter? What key evidence supports this point? Go to the article about the Battle of Midway at the website below. Find a quote from the website that supports the chapter's main point.

BATTLE OF MIDWAY

abdocorelibrary.com/world-war-ii-pacific

CHAPTER FOUR

US VICTORIES IN 1945

Battles in the Pacific theater continued into 1945. General Douglas MacArthur used an island-hopping technique. These were amphibious attacks on islands throughout the Pacific. Ships landed near the shores of islands, which allowed US marines and soldiers to storm the islands' beaches. US naval and air strikes then aided these attacks.

US troops used many types of vehicles for amphibious landings. These vehicles could be used on the ground and in the water.

THE BATTLE OF IWO JIMA

Iwo Jima, also called Iō Island, lies south of mainland Japan. On February 19, 1945, the US military launched an amphibious attack as part of its island-hopping campaign. Capturing the mountainous island would allow US planes to gain a base for bombing campaigns on Japan's main islands. Iwo Jima is just 760 miles (1,220 km) from Tokyo, Japan.

Lieutenant General Kuribayashi Tadamichi organized Japan's defense. Aboveground, he called for the construction of buildings to provide coverage from gunfire. He also ordered the Japanese military to dig a network of tunnels so that Japanese soldiers could hide underground. He planned to make use of Iwo Jima's caves too. These hiding spots would force US troops to engage the Japanese in close combat.

Major General Harry Schmidt led the US Marine Corps in the invasion. He tasked the marines to claim the peak of Mount Suribachi. Mount Suribachi is one of the highest points on Iwo Jima. If marines were

Joe Rosenthal took a photograph of the moment when marines reached the top of Mount Suribachi on February 23, 1945. It is one of the most famous photos taken during World War II.

able to reach this point, it would mean that they had successfully pushed past Japanese defenses. The marines secured the location on February 23. But fighting on the island continued until March 26.

The Navajo code talkers were instrumental to US success at Iwo Jima. They were a group of 29 Diné (Navajo) men who coded and decoded US military messages. The code was based on the Diné language. Before switching to this code system, it took about 30 minutes to translate three lines of code. Since it was their own native language, the Navajo code talkers could translate three lines of the code they developed in seconds. During the Battle of Iwo Jima, they sent and decoded approximately 800 messages.

KAMIKAZE TACTICS

Japanese pilots had used kamikaze tactics in other battles during World War II, but they heavily employed this form of attack at Okinawa. During kamikaze attacks, pilots fly their planes directly into a target, such as a ship. This severely damages the ship, but the pilots are killed. More than 1,000 kamikaze attacks occurred during the Battle of Okinawa. The Japanese government believed it was worthwhile to sacrifice planes and people to damage US ships. Japanese pilots were told they were sacrificing their lives for the emperor.

Navajo code talkers often traveled with marine units in the field. They communicated over radios to pass coded messages to and from their unit.

Although the United States was victorious at Iwo Jima, the human cost of the battle was high. It was one of the bloodiest battles in US Marine Corps history. Nearly 7,000 US troops were killed. The Japanese military suffered even heavier losses. Approximately 22,000 Japanese soldiers and sailors died at Iwo Jima. The Battle of Iwo Jima showed that Japan would not surrender easily.

THE BATTLE OF OKINAWA

Okinawa is a large island that lies south of mainland Japan. It was the site of the last major battle of the

PERSPECTIVES

THE FIREBOMBING OF TOKYO

The US military flew B-29 bombers to Japan from Iwo Jima. On March 10, 1945, the US military launched a bombing campaign against Tokyo, Japan. US B-29 bombers dropped about 1,500 tons (1,360 metric tons) of firebombs on the city. It was the deadliest air raid in history. Historians estimate that as many as 100,000 people died in the bombing, many of whom were civilians. Katsumoto Saotome was 12 years old on the night of the firebombing. In 2020, he spoke about that night. He said, "For a child who did not know the true meaning of death or fear, March 10 was my first experience of that."

Pacific theater. Taking over Okinawa would allow the US military to more easily target Japan's main islands by plane. It also gave the US Navy the ability to block supplies from reaching Japan.

More than 60,000 US troops landed on Okinawa's shores when the invasion began on April 1, 1945. The British Royal Navy supported the US Navy. The British helped limit Japanese air activity.

BATTLES IN THE PACIFIC

This map shows the locations of key battles that occurred in the Pacific theater of World War II. How does this map help you understand the text?

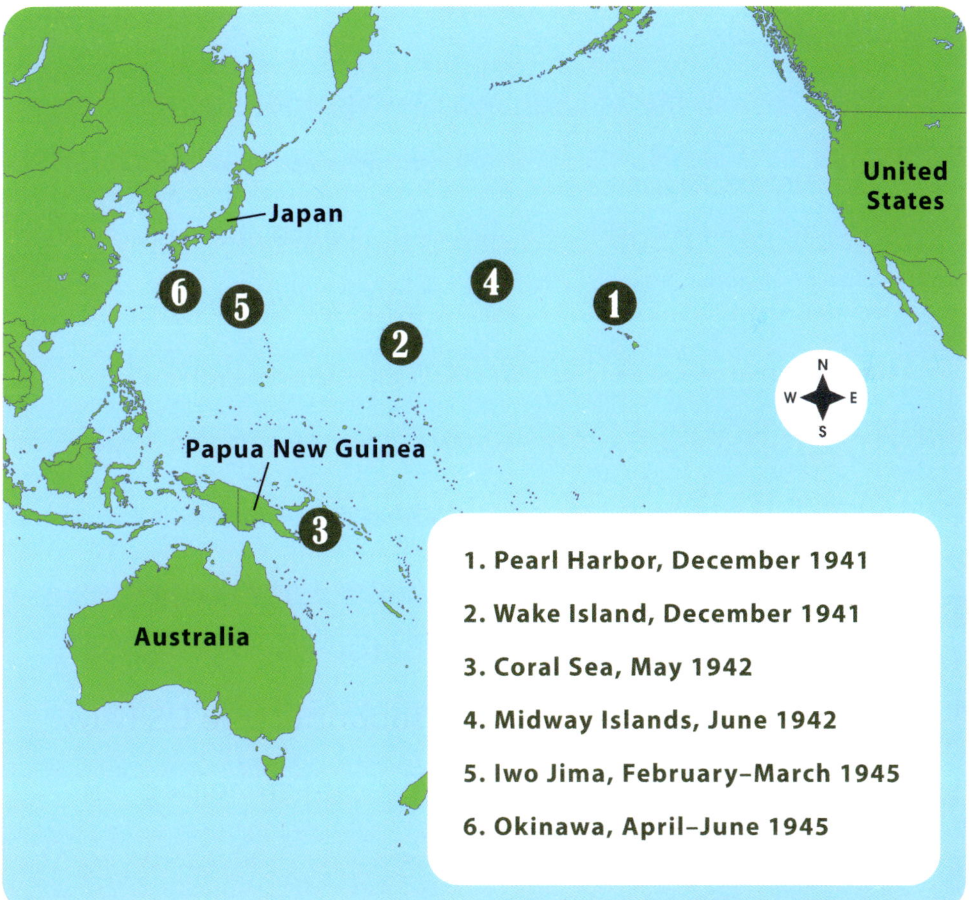

The Japanese military planned to stall US troops at Okinawa. This way Japan would have time to build up defenses on its major islands. The fighting continued until June 22. The Japanese military forced the US military to use up a lot of resources. In total, the US military dropped approximately 521,000 bombs on Okinawa and fired more than 600,000 rounds of ammunition.

The loss of life at Okinawa was staggering. The US military suffered approximately 49,000 casualties. This included 12,500 dead or missing soldiers. Many more were injured and could no longer fight. Historians estimate that as many as 110,000 Japanese soldiers and 150,000 Japanese civilians were killed during this battle. After the battle, it was unclear when the war would end and how many more people would be killed before Japan surrendered.

STRAIGHT TO THE SOURCE

A memorial in Arizona celebrates the Navajo code talkers. Thomas H. Begay, a Navajo code talker, spoke about his unit during a gathering in August 2022. He said:

> *During . . . World War II, the Navajos had developed the best code that was never broken by the enemy of the United States of America. It was the hardest thing to learn, but we were able to develop a code that cannot be broken by the enemy.*

Source: Suelen Rivera. "Navajo Code Talker Commemorates National Holiday at Arizona Memorial." *KTAR News*, 14 Aug. 2022, ktar.com. Accessed 21 Aug. 2023.

POINT OF VIEW

After reading this quote, think about Begay's point of view on the Navajo code talkers. What is your point of view about this unit's role in the war? Write a short essay explaining how your point of view is similar to or different from Begay's. Explain why.

CHAPTER FIVE

ENDING THE WAR

The Japanese military faced heavy losses at Iwo Jima and Okinawa. Although Japan's ally, Germany, had surrendered on May 7, 1945, the Empire of Japan did not appear to be anywhere close to surrender. US military planners considered an invasion of Japan, but this would extend the fighting in the Pacific. In July 1945, US military planners estimated that an invasion would result in 1.7 to 4 million more US casualties.

Millions of Japanese troops and civilians had died by the end of the Battle of Okinawa. This included approximately 3,800 kamikaze pilots.

J. Robert Oppenheimer, *third from left*, was one of many scientists who worked on the Manhattan Project.

THE MANHATTAN PROJECT

Scientists in the United States had been working on a powerful new type of weapon since 1942. It was the atomic bomb. US policymakers believed that a weapon of this power could end the war in Japan without an invasion that would risk US lives.

The Manhattan Project was the name of the government-funded research project that developed an atomic weapon. J. Robert Oppenheimer led a major project site in Los Alamos, New Mexico. Scientists at Los Alamos studied nuclear energy. The nucleus is the center of an atom. Fission is the act of splitting an atom's nucleus. It creates massive amounts of energy. Atomic weapons harness energy created by the fission of uranium or plutonium atoms. The scientists working on the Manhattan Project developed the most powerful explosives the world had ever seen.

TESTING THE ATOMIC BOMB

On July 16, 1945, Oppenheimer tested the first atomic bomb at a New Mexico test site called Trinity. The bomb was dropped 100 feet (30 m) from the top of a tower in the desert. There was a flash of light as the bomb detonated. A mushroom-shaped cloud billowed upward from the explosion site. The extreme heat from the explosion caused the desert sand to turn to glass in an 800-yard (730-m) radius.

Franklin D. Roosevelt was the US president at the start of World War II. But he died before the war ended. His vice president, Harry S. Truman, became president on April 12, 1945. After US scientists successfully tested an atomic bomb on July 16, Truman was forced to make the difficult decision about whether to use this weapon against Japan.

Ultimately Truman decided to use the atomic bomb. He believed it had the potential to end the war without additional risk to the US military. Along with world leaders in the United Kingdom and China, Truman issued the Potsdam Declaration on July 26, 1945. The declaration called for Japan to surrender or face destruction. Eleven days later, Japan still had not surrendered. The US military prepared to drop an atomic bomb on Japan.

DROPPING THE BOMBS

The US Army Air Forces (AAF) dropped an atomic bomb called Little Boy on the Japanese city of Hiroshima on August 6, 1945. US military planners targeted Hiroshima because it was a Japanese military headquarters and a port city. When Japan did not immediately surrender, the AAF dropped a second bomb, called Fat Man, on August 9. The original target was Kokura. But the

ATOMIC BOMB STATISTICS

HIROSHIMA

The atomic bomb Little Boy was dropped on August 6, 1945. Approximately 80,000 people died instantly from the bombing.

NAGASAKI

The atomic bomb Fat Man was dropped on August 9, 1945. Approximately 40,000 people were immediately killed.

This map shows the cities that the US military targeted with atomic bombs. How does this information help you understand the effects of dropping the bombs?

city was covered by clouds that day. Instead, the AAF targeted Nagasaki. Nagasaki was another port city with military facilities.

The aftermath of the bombs was extreme. In Hiroshima, 5 square miles (13 sq km) of the city were completely destroyed. Immediately, more than 80,000 people were killed. In Nagasaki, approximately

PERSPECTIVES

SURVIVING HIROSHIMA

The atomic bomb destroyed about 63 percent of Hiroshima's buildings. Historical sites were destroyed by the bomb, including Hiroshima Castle. Japanese writer Yoko Ota survived the bombing. She wrote about how she felt when she realized the castle was destroyed. "My heart shook like a great wave," she wrote. "The grief of stepping over the corpses of history pressed upon my heart."

40,000 people were instantly killed when the bomb exploded there. The civilian death toll of these bombs was massive.

The atomic bombs also had long-term effects on people in the cities. Uranium and plutonium are radioactive elements. These types of materials can have dangerous short- and long-term health effects. By the end of 1945, about 210,000 people were killed as a result of the atomic bombs dropped on Hiroshima and Nagasaki. Survivors also faced increased risks of cancer and other radiation-related illnesses.

JAPAN SURRENDERS

Japan surrendered on August 15, 1945. The official documents of surrender were signed on September 2. The war in the Pacific was finally over. This marked the end of World War II.

Japan had pushed the United States to enter the war. But Japan's initial strategy of a quick defeat at Pearl Harbor was not achieved. The cost of life was high for Japan and the United States, which led to the United States' use of atomic bombs to end the war.

EXPLORE ONLINE

Chapter Five discusses the United States' decision to drop atomic bombs on Hiroshima and Nagasaki. The article at the website below goes into more depth on this topic. Does the article answer any of the questions you had about President Truman's decision?

TRUMAN AND THE ATOMIC BOMB

abdocorelibrary.com/world-war-ii-pacific

IMPORTANT DATES

December 7, 1941

The Empire of Japan attacks Pearl Harbor. More than 2,400 Americans are killed in the attack. The US Congress declares war against Japan on December 8.

December 11, 1941

Japanese naval ships arrive at Wake Island. Wake Island falls to Japan on December 23.

May 4, 1942

The Battle of the Coral Sea begins. The battle ends on May 8, with the US Navy successfully defending the port.

June 3, 1942

The Battle of Midway begins. The United States wins the battle on June 6.

February 19, 1945

The US military launches an amphibious attack on Iwo Jima. The fighting continues until March 26 and results in thousands of deaths on both sides.

April 1, 1945
US troops land on the shores of Okinawa. By the time the battle ends on June 22, more than 270,000 people have been killed in the fighting.

August 1945
The US military drops an atomic bomb on Hiroshima on August 6. US forces drop a second bomb on Nagasaki on August 9. Japan surrenders on August 15.

September 2, 1945
The United States and Japan sign documents of Japan's surrender, and World War II officially ends.

STOP AND THINK

Tell the Tale

Chapter One of this book describes the attack on Pearl Harbor. Imagine you are at Pearl Harbor on the day of the attack. Write 200 words about what you see and hear. How would you want the government to respond to the attack?

Surprise Me

Chapter Four discusses the battles of Iwo Jima and Okinawa. After reading this book, what two or three facts about World War II battles in the Pacific did you find most surprising? Write a few sentences about each fact. Why did you find each fact surprising?

Take a Stand

President Truman decided to drop atomic bombs on both Hiroshima and Nagasaki. These attacks ended the war and limited the number of US lives lost in battle. However, the bombs killed hundreds of thousands of Japanese civilians and caused long-term health effects. Do you agree that US forces should have dropped the bombs? Why or why not?

Another View

This book talks about the importance of the 1942 Battle of Midway in the Pacific theater. As you know, every source is different. Ask a librarian or another adult to help you find another source about this event. Write a short essay comparing and contrasting the new source's point of view with that of this book's author. What is the point of view of each author? How are they similar and why? How are they different and why?

GLOSSARY

ally
a nation working with another nation to achieve a common goal

amphibious
related to both land and water

casualty
a person wounded or killed in battle

colony
an area under the control of a foreign country

embargo
a ban on trading with another country

empire
a group of countries or territories ruled by one leader or government

infamy
an evil reputation

intercept
to secretly receive communication meant for someone else

radioactive
relating to harmful particles produced by certain elements

theater
an area where battles happen

ONLINE RESOURCES

To learn more about World War II in the Pacific, visit our free resource websites below.

Core Library CONNECTION
FREE! COMMON CORE MULTIMEDIA RESOURCES

Visit **abdocorelibrary.com** or scan this QR code for free Common Core resources for teachers and students, including vetted activities, multimedia, and booklinks, for deeper subject comprehension.

Booklinks NONFICTION NETWORK
FREE! ONLINE NONFICTION RESOURCES

Visit **abdobooklinks.com** or scan this QR code for free additional online weblinks for further learning. These links are routinely monitored and updated to provide the most current information available.

LEARN MORE

Carser, A. R. *The US Decision to Drop the Atomic Bomb*. Abdo, 2022.

Daddis, Susan, and Michelle Jovin. *World War II in the Pacific*. Teacher Created Materials, 2020.

INDEX

About the Author

Angela Lim is an MFA student in poetry at Indiana University in Bloomington, Indiana.